Zam Bonk Dip

JONTY TIPLADY grew up in Doncaster, South Yorkshire, leaving to study literature and philosophy in London, Paris, then Brighton, receiving a Ph.D. in French philosophy from University of Sussex. He has published eight pamphlets of poetry, including *Zam Bonk Dip* (Barque Press, 2007) and *At The School Of Metaphysics* (Fly By Night, 2008). He is also the author, with Sarah Wood, of a study of the poetry of Wallace Stevens: *The Blue Guitar* (Artwords Press, 2007). He won the 2009 Crashaw Prize and currently lives in London.

Zam Bonk Dip

by

JONTY TIPLADY

SALT

LONDON

PUBLISHED BY SALT PUBLISHING
Dutch House, 307–308 High Holborn, London WC1V 7LL United Kingdom

© Jonty Tiplady, 2010

Salt Publishing 2010

Printed in Great Britain by the MPG Books Group, Bodmin and King's Lynn

Typeset in Swift 9.5 / 13

ISBN 978 1 84471 737 8 paperback

1 3 5 7 9 8 6 4 2

Contents

Acknowledgements

The ten poem sequence 'Zam Bonk Dip' was first published as a pamphlet by Barque Press in 2007. 'At The School Of Metaphysics' was published by Fly By Night in 2008. Parts of 'The Broken Heart' appeared in *Hot Gun 2* and on *onedit*.

'Delirium is not usually tender, hallucination is not easily kind. Cartoons don't often succeed in making sadism irrealisable in a specifically human heart. The three dimensions of most objects are hardly a triptych at all, their fourth and up rarely if ever a chamber music infolding unlistenable loss. Most things don't hurt like they do inside, or sing like the love they must yet have of us. This book by the person Jonty Tiplady, patient and impetuous, wild and soft, disjointed and palatial, will: as fragile as our clarity itself.'

—KESTON SUTHERLAND

Zam Bonk Dip

1

Alight here, and see how it steps backwards.
How can it not, since in the storm
coming, not in my land but on that horizon,
all kind of monsters, jumbos and jumpers,
Frank says this, the big yellow rabbit,
the mystical bunny, for you know it is he,
oh Jonny Lee, put away the foil,
for a storm is coming, a storm, a storm,
a storm that will swallow all the children,
send all the children flying, over there!,
and only the Bowie bird, the car-
ping fish, the *c'est de l'or, vent d'est,* the beet-
root stained vest, the Sean Barker king, the come--
lately fling, and all the other world games, and cosmo
zeros, and new and old planets, the storms in the
eaves, will put us, Nanny and Bruce and Bill,
all shivery tots, and antelope blues, all crashing
bang together again.

For silly automatic theory
answer yes. My body says yes, my house says
yes, my tree on the horizon line behind
my house says yes. I am living,
in my soul's soul, in the soul that lives
like a wisp of smoke above my own wigwam, in the
age of the answer, in the ageless age of
my pen, my pen that never comes
a cropper, *dept-rayon*, that never flaps, cartoon
beauty, that never kips, Mr Flying Bike, that never laps
me, for I lap it, we lap the one the other, in the same
white chalk ring, Mr Hangman, that never even takes
refuge in
                    not even once, not even a mite of it.
What I find in insider psyche, nothing grows fusty in this
a tad, this tad of, this old giant tardis butterfly man.

3

Rivers of milk, rivers of trees, anoint the
blobject beckoning on the Olympic Stadium, its milk
spotlights fanning the blancmange crescents.
Look out the micro chip stripes in the jello
like starless stars. Fan through too the baby gods
in the skyscraper arch. The old sad baby drinks up that
brown carpet milk, swims in the toy visions. His oscular
pinks turn. The tiny tinny toy army marches on
his head. It was at this point fire flowered from
his belly, and his hands began to stone crumble. Still
he had the start of precognitive powers in the milk.

4

The early prince licked her all over.
Sailor Milan had fits or something like this
and said I cannot even tie a bow.
He could not pick up a two penny piece either.
The other two came back in the second film
and the key for the suitcase in the tarmac
drew new water out.

Or rage as ordered in digits in Tokyo. I have been like the paradise pig for so long, with my turbo credits always nearly out, my self bad for my self. And I'll be like it for a while still, or even longer, since the rissole always is. Yet with a sprig behind my oinky ear, a grey Silvestre patch on my eye, a Popeye wink and a winning way with the dead, I will make like with the angry ones and raise them like baked beans. Microtic gods, bless my ditz with your nipples dragged in yen milk and I will take Abi Cadabby by the pig tails singing *Yes it was I forgot it was woes wot count. Saw you the clown trample out the stars though, because of his hate? Saw you pig the Lilly toy with worse when she could have insisted the best because of her hate? I am sick, sick to the tiptoes of this conundrum, with pieces of hate. Did Charley twine the stars on his fingers because of hate? Is heaven in pieces because of hate? Is Whitney Churchill fucked by the bad man Bobby Brown because of hate? Did you ever see Charley gnaw on his hat for that? What is the 'key in a kiss' he spoke of, anyway? Because of hate? As sure as eggs are eggs, and as sure as I eat my hat, if the Good Lord let me hate I will tell you soon.*

6

Imagine Bucci is right and this little o
is sore and the only spare spot for miles, that
there is no new milk for gillions, and sand in
your sandwich eye. After that final
no, a yes beyond yeses and noes
on which the future of the daily planet depends
like gums on teeth, like I want to do everything simple
there is for it. Yet I take only the blebbiest
of spinaches, fall into the cosmic disbelief
of the wimpling, the bulbs all glacial
                              ice cube bolts

        even Rocky's new body cannot crap thunderbolts
and Poopdeck Papa is no longer master
of the spinach domain. But cosmic disbelief I may never
believe. 'Wonder no world deny may...'
Stet. This morning I started making porridge
with water and rice syrup for the first time.

In the rat palais, with the frowns of a thousand
chip teddies, I comes like the simple one simply done.
No order here, and so no need. Tell of eyes still
galactic, the fizz at their lids, the treacle
treacling together like arctic glue, the cinnamon
darts, the rink. Milk's secrets she kept close by her in her
mountain hut in the grass desert, the suitcase dumped
with the straws and other crap. I believed she was
Olympic. Then she only went and died
on me. You know she's still my cub though
for good. We may even fall in love again
even though it's a thing of the past.

8

Beyond error's sea, with the starres
on Zane's Zorro mask. It started, to start
again, stepping back, with wanting to live
in Casablanca. Sun lights, cannonballs
running to fetch your window blossom
on the stem. All I want to write is the word
ricci. You can not still be at the breakfast
bar, save may it be so.

9

Arf, ark, that's right, killer me this way kill me
that, it's all the same. Start again as you must, fresh balloon and foil,
crease the forager, maim this magpie, mainly
wonder, weather, mouths open, incidental
Choy. Gee Johnny, gee Choy! Nobody ever singsong
it ever so softly, like a micro tongue, as you did in the
Big Bad West. Play with the felt, as Jet said, play with
the felts. Make heavenhell of a trap, as nobody said,
make hell of a highwater by plane.
Toughen up too! In the beginning, in Virginia, in 1607, and in
1988, the whole world was America, more so than it is now,
and it's still like that, the ballpark is my soul,
the soup sprig messes up. Make this one, Giant Donny,
the biggest step backwards yet, the big old step
backwards. Play dead, as if the whole
thoroughfare. My American, it's the dim sunniest thing I
saw, on the old northern ridge, on the racer, in the
answer phone age, after the sports stars, book words,
geography and science words.

10

It's always time to sing again
careless soul. Error laughs error's socks
off, let's record everything in Sunshine Hotel.

Manic Milk

Kittitian dawn, light sabres on the mountain top.

≈

Scally wally, wag.

≈

There must be, I thought to myself one afternoon, a funny bone heaven.

≈

Ricci is out back. She called for you twice all day. She tried your boots on. When she asks you for the apple, remember to say what I have taught you to say. Yes.

≈

If I write letters on the world, Dindane, will you forgive me? I don't know, Jonny Turps, but find yourself a place to sit uncomfortably while I open up the suitcase.

≈

Martha has a blackboard in her room and comes in from work freezing with pangs and pangs. She has magazine all ready for the bath. I must to the pet shop this weekend she says in the bath. I must find the Bassett for Stan.

≈

[15]

Let a rainbow ripen a syllable crescent in your belly.

≈

Words pinked out of the air, and yet suddenly it's all cold.
The whole hundred are so cold.

≈

The booby-trapped egg, the secret on your body.

≈

Bugs Bunny burning.

Float Away Milk Bath

1

Egg bouillon, G. sings to
her letters, Gad and Pearl.
The pearl jacket in *apricari*.
In a sort of complex or hotel,
in an animal factory for crackers
in Philly, I sketch ampersand flowers
resembling your smalls
for the last time.
   Notice the *el* in camel.

2

Tarzan (who Rocky imitated in the zoo) learned to draw
by looking at the ants anting on his celastasia. My pocket
branch is cracking, breakfast words, the letterbox of lids, the
kangaroo, the daddy m, the cracking *el* in *elMêmesternal*.

3

Drunkenly neat it's writ
by the page. Suck micro thunder
off it the page. More than a duke
trying to stay afloat, a sailor
works on the flow in
         his battleship.
He whistles in the dark.
Softly, in your dreams, the angered song
the little boy softly faints sings.

[17]

Clyde, left turn, loves me to love him a
sings
to love me. It's animal love
all together now.

A

In the heart of the geek elastic zoo rip chords attach me beyond shears and sheepishness. You the *Bon Bonbonnière* air of believe as nobody would have dared think. Meanwhile at the conker exchange, some monkey business, a man on the roof with an air rifle. *Just a minute, I have an important matter to attend to in Rome.* To the soul-coloured one, to the rhubarb triangle, to the cutlery. You were so beautifully sheepish now I come to think of it.

B

I remember how
I mixed my perfect friends' bitternesses
with my own
and that I love you, through to pieces
of heaven
right in the middle of my life,
lifelong I mean, lifewise
in this absolute
kerfuffle I make
to spill you my astral
blood
sugar—

give me my conker back.

Both beat at love
beat me at love
(hug the blade)
& I'll know how to forget.

≈

Soft graces
sent up
ones that swim
gobbles
confused
anonyghosts
as well as particulars.

≈

Sublime TV
brown pouffe
house quiet
in bowls
drinking
each other's
piss, did we ever
do that
even with
party hats on.

At The School Of Metaphysics

Madrock Gunned Down In Flowers

Here is where my chickens began to unhatch, where
furiously hopeful music dug me down like it dug me down
before. The bruising I had been cruising for
was worse still, it was a flirt with sort of an evil twist, cassettes
of Casualty videotaped at the weekend
in my pockets. I was averse, I was bad placed, I was feeling
more and more channelled by Amy Winehouse
who sang you are so down down
it's like hanging a rope suspended over
the only eyes in the world you could never compare. Here, then,
must be elsewhere. Here the moon's not asleep
and a sinkhole eats up the neighbourhood as wildebeests
die struggling to get out. Here I'm not in love with Rio,
and the Tweedy bird downloads on the frosted train. Here I'm over pop,
which therefore rises falls again, like there is no absence only very weak
shades of presence down to the custard at your feet
and antireverie. I learnt this back at the school of metaphysics
where repression is eternal, punkie, and affirmation succeeds. It can be felt
like fetching a pocketful of crumbly earth fire up from the ugly moon
peak. We still have a certain love of presence, it's only just begun. Was it
too beautiful that the gamers in separate lounges and chillers also were
kings whose widows buried themselves at their deaths? This is school
and if I say it, it clips its hands sourly with a recharge
of affirmation. I can affirm that, I can affirm
nothing sadly but got a bean, that I'm losing so much
especially zeros, the hot ones I put here to prove life isn't
something we made up.

Sahara Ha Ha

Reynols takes hold the drums
at three. He has formed this band
before they were born. Reynols, where are you
on the ocean bed where there is a glass full of
ocean. You are like the dumbo octopus, but only
funnier. Every night billions of sea creatures swim thousands
of metres or so up to the photic zone. You are whichever
a light psyche like them. In Rio they have concert now
and wonder keeps tearing

round. We will destroy you for silly, says Reynols, who are the
only band in the world. Reynols writes postcards and they
are the only ones. He writes songs and they
are they play with your love. They are the best on Planeta Sardina, too
early for your eyes. Wonder keys keeps tearing around a
chamame tape. America does not exist
and his friendship tambourine advanced. Beyond Mexico there is
the sea only the sea

ha ha. Reynols is the type who when you cut your leg
or his he says how beautiful. In the bottom of the sea they have
lots of love. The band is formed of three of them. M. Jackson on double
bass, Chi Crespo on double bass, and Cucak Ijo on double bass. Or,
M. Jackson on hi-hat and Chi on computer hand. I
myself am the genius that formed this band. The others
are a mess, some of them queers. When Reynols
is drunk he

is not the stupid one, he is the happy one. A happiness he cannot
face. He shares it in shreds, says a little dance and kicks
Jackson's arse. We have all played TV with Reynols since

we were ten. Reynols is like that. He proposes
a kind of revolutionary bearsdoor, and does books
for girls. *Time to kiss dead the net tyrants*
in your mind as the keys slip up out of your pocket
music yeah music weak sometimes the sound of bricks
envelopes you.

Eskimo Porn Belt

Like a grass burn in space, like a virtual joy-bender, like a mad head smashing bits of stuff, like look a pop-up erection book!, like I myself have three penises, two hard, one soft, one for the beach, just in case, the flying saucers, like switch to manual, wow the rat dies, like nothing but hound dogs.

Like God who Prince said was a traitor, like little and large in leisure suits, like it ain't gonna suck itself, like switch to the manual, like monkey reclining, that's what we find different now the mechanism of death.

Like old phones rock different in space, switch to manual, like go back to weekend feather school for free, like go ahead sit on my poem, like watch dog electric support scores a double zero, utah, domino, chew on this, saint legs juice.

Like sputters of pink, like I have a micro colourful new C3PO pants with exquisite species under white water caps sacs and a conveyor belt and ball-buster kit for a ratchet clang, like I myself have my own big dictionary, and in it Jimmy says don't compare you'll despair or use other language it sounds better.

Like tissue for some universal fucking soul beat, tippo, teach snow, get your human ass/night on, like I'm going off!, I was really very pleased when I did that duck.

Like Devon and Miles and Michael and yes Lisa and Abi and Cadabby and Manky I mean Banky Moon, like pull back my trousers, like you make goal posts for my sugar, like slip in the snow monkey metaphor with an e softly but firmly, like look how little large is.

Like can you get me a copy of your penis, like you understand the women body thing, like put on your Eskimo porn belt, don't touch the green square, like fun fur like orange fun, like fun was taking over the planet, like I think I might be able to get you some work down there.

Like little spanners rising and shining, like don't do what Donny does, like Jimmy does it, like Miles does it, like ants are back in, like I wear swastika pants, on the stars on the floor, like I wear orange and red fur, like you fucking chess fag, like spring in my anus, like summer in yours, like sleepy animals that don't make phone calls, like Buffo only emerged when you stopped sex and gooed her back together, like cherries popping in the, like smudge pudding, like sledge hammering your pinko, like a jam jar, drinking from a jar, like wow get your sheep dog nose on, like no point not loving just better to love, simple, like don't be like that duck, like it's thirsty work being daffety.

Like avalanche lilies, like the silk road online between us, like laugher goo on your ass, like fucking the future, like abracafuckingsexdabra, like happiness things, like gags and crams, like sword palace, like otemesando, like a little more, pudding duck, like smutly it cedes away from the deck, like, like the gold boy runs out of berries in the straw, like juice the brick, like rodeo beasts gathered round, an old haunted heart sputtered, a giant shiver, a wanky moon, like milk her over the bedchamber made milk-made, set her to the milk tune star, presto, a dark kisses it off, like sexember, like I believe you thousands wouldn't.

For The Brazilian Rocket Queen

Live minor America you are in my soul rock babe
in the alchemist who sent you to the corner. They sent you to the corner
with cheese muffs debonair. You
you go play with the forty yards. You go swing,
you go do the twist again. How can
you weigh an invisible phantom weight on the pin-prick
bone sticking out the centre of my chest. Through inclusion
omit you half tender sleepy seal. Deep down I can't make sense, it
was like you were as ugly B-E-A-U-T-I-F-U-L as the moon and
I was laden with crisps and yet was so happy to be
there again, with you in darkest happiness, and be mine. I have not
said as was, never will, never will transform, for the more
I might the more it would, and omit again. I must be scared
that happiness is like this, its
magic study a grizzle-pit half the time. It's like when my room
resembles a hospital, my insides cry out, and
the thing seems to be the more happy I am
I went with my Mum to headbutt a cactus. How are you the love
of my life in different Google machine language. Dream a little
brief dream, under a wheelying rainbow. Those lava mice are scathing
about every poem's end.

Dear World And Everyone In It

I'm Mister Lonely now myself, on a thrashing stretcher. I'm alive like white kids imitating black kids imitating white kids. Feathers foam out of my mouth, ginger trains, the truth, etc. I met this girl the other day, she had a nice ass. I wanted to titfuck that ass. I wanted to titfuck that ass all night long. I wanted to titfuck that ass with my ass all night long. I wanted to titfuck that ass with your ass all night long. I wanted, with Alex Treebeck and his photo of a giraffe during an earthquake, to titfuck that ass with my ass and your ass all night long, etc. I eventually spoke to this girl. I asked her if she remembered that bit in *ET* where the flying BMX bike is silhouetted against the moon. It made me want to cry, I said, and not know whether life or death was preferable, but then since there is choice, and since it's a matter of preference, you could only *prefer* life, that's what *preference* is, *this* preference, and that, even though this was almost impossible, you had to multiply images from its point of view. She looked at me gone out. I said perhaps you don't even like ET. She smiled a bit and said yes she *quite* liked ET, but not as much as she liked me. This made me happy for a while but then I got restless and went on *Facebook* and saw that ET had twelve trillion friends. I just couldn't get myself back together after that. Or rather, I realised I'd better get myself back together, and start complicating everything, but I fell asleep for a week, and forgot even that. If you asked me what I believe, I would say something like the following. I believe (1) that we need more affirmation. We need, as Roy Scheider might have it, *a bigger affirmation*. For example: already in 19 and 44 purple dash snow someday there will be another love to the end or just a coca-cola a day allowing me to love what I love and hate what I hate. I believe (2) that we are moving closer to the sun.

The proof of this is in that everything is starting to get very yellow. I believe (3) that you may as well fall in love with a leaf. I believe (4, 5 and 6) that discos love ecstasy, echo is still with his bunnymen, and that you were always looking pretty good today. I believe (7) that this is too sad because too deathless. I believe (8) that we are like the child who sits on a wind which rips apart the blood and imagines itself seeing itself from above on a flooded earth and so no longer cares what it says. I believe (9) that it's all about doing everything once and then moving on, but that you can always go back to do it again, and that this return takes place *in the midst of* what you can never really know you moved beyond or into. I believe (10) that it's daft to say there is no more this or that (street corner soul, for example) since it assumes there once was (a sort of *historical euphoric recall*), and this lets in a kind of contraband nostalgia even worse than the one presumably being diminished. So I believe (11) that since there still must be *some* street corner soul, for example, some *effects* of it, the issue becomes not loss but the quality of these surviving effects as they enigmatically insist *out of* and *into* that loss, in which case street corner soul was perhaps always *not* what we think we now know it isn't anymore, which perhaps means it *now* has a chance of being more itself than ever it was, more snappy and strange, which is to say less, *always less*; yet anewly so. I believe in the toy synthesizer approach (12), in Billy Mitchell's switch from Pac-Man to hot sauce (this tells us a lot about 9, 10 and 11) (13), and in positively failed beauty (14). I believe (15), dear world and everyone in it, that I spend a lot of time trying to replace this Napoleon hood with a clock of rainbows just in case, but failing. Napoleon, after all, is just another way of being nobody, of being beaten up in gold. I believe (16) that Nicholas

Royle, also, enters into heaven. Last but not least I believe, as the song says, that you are the only one to understand why it is I will have to spend a lifetime saying the opposite of what I believe, which is that there is no such thing as cosmic pessimism because there will be nobody there to feel it, unless there is somebody there to feel it, or unless there is nobody or somebody here, now, to feel it. Are we not a little this last glissade made colossal pop affirmation?

The Triangle Fire At 19/11

Almost even too free and fair to want to
act as art at all, since that is always trading
on wounds, making an insubstantial you
something for somebody else, two-bit beauty
or its counterproof.

Another mother earth sets off. If only the cats and
dogs would vomit me I mean love me let me
snug snugly to what you cannot do, to love itself do
carrying out our birth. Our glorious body still to
come.

Thirst Pockets

YOU filled
the square
with words
to get into
the room
now watch this move.

TOMORROW love
a catatonic
affirmation
will ravish
the sleep
beam.

EVIL Cho
will rise &
shine
&
kill
36
fractal
ducks.

DUSK dandles
& rodeo beasts
catch wind tracks
east.

STAR-SHINER
in the vaginal crest
babbling.

CRYSTAL infant
growing
face
almost magic,
tongue flicks
the ball bag.

HIT the one
in the middle
while Burt Young
fingers Duke's
face.

THE girl-star
macarooned
sold out by
the underclass
gradually.

BASIC signs
called back
from the brink.

GO inland
amber-ember-empire
hey how else.

ESKIMO sneezes
strawberry cuts
life is not so short.

THE false negative
unhappiness
overalloyed
funny how
don't be
like that
duck.

THE big house
of the rolling
exorcism
the gifted city,
i'll be back
soon.

REVENGE
drops
worded
backwards
colour
fucked &
hyped
into place,
an haut
boy
tingling
from the shit
kicked out.

TEETH clones
rock on
zombie
pedals
pressed
dush goes the gore
the shoe
or else
i'll fade away.

TA
for the mercies
universes
flame thrown
into a
baby mystery
dumb & cuffed
as itself
opens itself
into a
there is so much.

RAIN snow
on me cruel
& soon relic
uncool
your negativity
skirt &
pink crown.

AND
anyhow
yeah
it's all
bollocks
we cannot
number clouds
i'm allbeleaved
for you.

THIRST pockets
break
in simple
books
somewhere over
under a
manky rainbow.

HE watched
the phone
too well
well a wing
& star
got the drop
on him
but anyway.

YOU only love
love twice
bedevilled
& if he dies
he dies
the heart-stop-spot
is fairer
than any
good
kicking.

A world clip
in the rear
mirror
with new
sunshine
vests
in the air
port.

MY last
house tape
of superroots
those shy
sly eyes
a primitive vision
of heart's desire.

THE wind has gone
i chew on my own
tongue.

HOLY family
blown away
awkward
like celery strings.

Tout

MY *Aoyun*
pink okra in the water cube

only a poem.

~

We kiss in the daytrip
free films
and cinema
(of you)
for everyone.

~

Beautiful like Danny Glover.

But it itself cuts out
like ribbons in sh-, not everything
is multipipelined by twists and bread,
and this nose hammer
in penny slits, goes
too.

≈

Little meta,
inside it love (loves)
only you.

≈

Remember
America? No,
me neither.

Like a sloth going backwards on a cross trainer.

∿

Reckon at last
that in pixels fair and fairly so hip
lassoed towards me, ta for absorbing
my unicorn fury.

∿

You,
little,
'my metaphysics',
a pain in my,
wii
altogether
'not bad as angels',
that century hard trash hardly
the sharpest pair of
coconuts.

All me writing in a way is Amorphophallusblaupunktism (in 'shivers') in ICI for 25 years.

[47]

Simple Phrases

Champagne was the first thing I drank. I like to dress as if my clothes are crying. I'm always crying. I'm always crying because deep down I fear I sometimes never loved the only one I ever really absolutely loved and now forget so I can love others, differently, more serenely, this possible impossibility life itself set up to the sound of love itself in the century airplane right until the end of the world whose sound it also is; THIS, this Broken Jonty Music, is (a) the 'it's too late when we die' and (b) 'THE LIVING YEARS' thought. I cry because I can't see this. I can't see this because I spent one hundred and fifty days on my balcony and forgot my flash visor. But sometimes I like optimistic dressing. My childhood is as follows. One day they all wanted a scrap so we all went to the park and we had a scrap but we ended up crying and kissing, especially the runner. We were crying and kissing especially the runner because we had a scrap but we didn't want a scrap. It's always like that. What I really wanted I went home and wrote straightaway but it only made the grisly crunch hook into me from which obviously flowers as stiff as bricks. The paper was blank. Do you want me to go and beat them up for you, she said. No, it's alright.

Give My Love To The Sunrise

Slow sand on frieze, pong factors in being happy, and what could be more beautiful than writing for those wolf children who come after the floods, inheriting only a taste for the 28 calendrical palms, and rendering everything, in a way, unclear? Unclear everything now, unclear that in spit and sandy bone we were given the message. No I didn't love you as you loved me, I loved you as I loved you. We burn towards toujours. Look how our hands reach us to ourselves. Look at the flight of the sea against the sea. You will be on me. I will die trying. So sad to be right.

Electrocuted by my own piss.

≈

Space out
these last vouchers, finger-searching the street. Glad
to be making limited progress. Everything
the frothy delight that goes into loving.
My extinction body tools.
How much I learned from you
a colossal pop affirmation.

≈

Actually the film is full of giants.

The Broken Heart

Sold Out The Ice Cream Van Today

Sold out the ice cream van today
                    and if it's that that makes me cry
            then sold out the van
                    ice pie in my chest something
            which my broke heart has
                    crumpled in the thrill
        its
                    pinger battery deletion
            deep inside the harrowing gone
                    administrator of the wind and windmills since
today impossible not to live you pass on.

Love Don't Like Me

Love don't like me
rain don't like me.

≈

Purple rain
thick teeth
soft cunt.

≈

No she in the woods
in the words
forget it.

≈

You don't
love me
you should.

≈

Your eyes
your tits
Christmas
all year round.

Black Funereal Cone

I awoke at S. and the magic crime of
absolute bereft air gulped her down. Really
the Summer does not start here.
Anyhow if I'm sleeping in the hardcore porn room for life,
then, well, then that's
April sorted at least. And May. And then
it's September. And it's December
(the day before Christmas eve is always so sad)
and I'm still in here, and then at least it
I'm still in here and
grinds me she wasn't worth a
well from invincible sadness you reboot love.

Wrong Answer

The over-broken jaw-hinge
of memory sellotaped up: the role that love plays in a lifetime
collapsing into you, *sunshine in a blackbox.*

Shut it, you
were talking into the receiver
and making speeches and that and
all the while there was nobody there.

Can you
say too true? In the toilet
would live with the mice, but imagine I'm your sister
or something, and wish I could give him a hug.

If love
was hurt?

In a word no. No need
for the nunnery resendings. Very important
the vertical blanking interrupt. People say let's die
they wrong.

                                                absolutely % your beauty

I think without you now
          as without myself
fear of a great counter-idealisation downfall
                    reason to
search me yet what will I ever be, me, if I had not been
madly loving and loved by you?

A dog barking surrounded by twigs brings tears to my eyes.

[56]

Hope Spasm

No accident this emergency how
on the keyboard
19 scarf what we at no scarf call
scarfing began scarfing in 19 scarfity scarf. Last will is
what recharged to nil stretch. But as you're cracking me up anyway
by the

  electric scene
  now so

over like life not love
in tiny rhythm bath the spaghettification of hope
only I could have hurt
by kind, magic pity surges
your animal thighs.

OOV

Anyhoo, come again. Not half. Eating
the simple, bored on the wing, why the flick, we, catch, e, ta, fat,
or even covered up the Nada dazzling Guanghua. Boring
boring: SlayerS_BoxeR vs. Oov is tasty mine. Undeniably soldiers of
the insane violence of the storm-crazy. Plus
boring boring, no flump colour. The *oov* in
iloveuoov means 'chosen one who shall cheat with the less resources'. Or,
on the light balls at the bottom of her highness. Or again, pull
your fingers off before I send you to the mountains with
many tender soldiers. Or, just maybe, cheater terran and crush
star last seen in a drophip holding hands at sunset. Dude, come on. In
dance shot pray at the junta. Standing flump. Anyhoo, hot bid, ta. Into
the sea. You fuck, you friggin pinhead, you yeti. Hey,
I was only wondering whether the Martians are still pretty.
Pensive and sweet, this boisterous passion, it creek, wearing an Olympia
Chaussettes football top in the early 80's. We miss
everyone. Mike, come back, play dirty and bad in nasty pink. Tasty mine,
come back. Franz Biberkopf come back. Blim Wit, Choi, Britney. At least
if that's going to be some white-on-white action around here, may it
be good, may it ramp. May it seize an z-rhythm. May it. However,
he seldom box and Zerg remembers the operation, or even
some inexplicable magic of small mistakes. Horse dip, fit mic, militaristic
red rope with gold rope. Pull
finger off, cra, na, crim, crim, crim,
slim-slim-slim-slim; *vroom*. FLANGE. Anyhoo, one
Halloween Lego Bucket coming up. We CAN win, the crazy gas demands
it, their nature. She even try fully grasp the rhythm sent over by
the troops. Boss Scags, don't. Even if no boxer king behind still change not

his weakness, nose down into joy. Anyhoo, after
the and of earth, three seconds, try on
a frock, pass it on and
LEAVE BRITNEY ALONE.

Julius Impossible

You answer
can't cope on one leg
with sanity kiss,
with mouth it would never just laugh
at love can make you happy.

∼

Half a year's sake
she scared of her face he love   .
the golden caviar good for it.

∼

I dreamt I was now so
I saw it film about your
cunt, mystic mania for.

∼

Marzipan rave,
telepathic moan,
poetic porn dubbed by the syndicate muse.

∼

Try not to sleep for the humid room:
the giddy thighs
under the duvet
wet tipped tendrils
and one dark shark fin to fold in.

∼

The ache of the starships,
the iteraphonic dream of the love flakes.

They Exist

Calxed by my own mood disorder pandemic
a suicide zest wasps my hand. Out of empathy for you
I develop a double lumbago. It's a right mess but
YOU SUCK MY THUMB and
it exists. Hold on
to the sentence while the coeval love grave turret we mean
tourretes love grace tourettes splashed cinderella lust forever and fur
and gloss
exists. I only ever knew you
to exist. There are others now thanks to you
who exist. The touching insuccess of your hand behind a closed door,
which exists.

Tout

As if what tout
   magic tout
      I will tout

but from the blue book
   (can't let go)
      my uncomfortable sleep

and the saddest thing I ever saw on a TV screen
   a bit of a let down that
      a bit let down

sleep with a bean bag between your knees
   LA VIE EN ROSE
      La vie en rose

'the soul of Paris'
   'we're all dead anyway' —
      FORGET THAT SHIT.

And what's with the uncomfortable sleep and everything anyway
   it's not like I broke
      'tender boot' 'SHE WAS FOOTBALL' (*Broken Heart* (2___))

except I did I absolutely did. The thing
   'was a cunt am no more but absolutely regret' that shit as if
      now da#fittesttweeterlol

  but who, really, ever gave a flying fuck about
    McLovin, Ballstack, dickmouth
      closely followed by beaver-gurus

since I was dying out there, I was
    totally in love with YOU ARE MY CENTURY and I can't let
        the pop song is

is says I can't let too I hear it still
    shy crime shine us of a century that lifted off sunshine
        slightly its hinges the corner of the room, I am

a Coriol 'too absolute', turned too wild
    and pretty like a soppy Saint
        I hurt you and, besides,

I've not had you here with me for some time.

You monkey only need direction change. A picaresque Buenosairean moves in another direction. Hope here a priori, laughter syllables. Love comes from where the birth of nick names comes, but still it makes me cry how you give wrong head to get a marksman to shoot me up. I do a pretty good impression myself, don't you think. The jump then is for lovesexiness since actually no I buy it all. I don't mind how bad it gets just as long as that yes (not a transcendental yes but a yes-flavoured-transcendental) is always there. There's more life if anything, and not without a scratch but a skuzzy starzy feeling. I confess first spills thrills of ill-loving, of making the beloved into a voodoo-thing, a thing-so-we-suffer. At least that was mascara blaspheming down my face with sweat. Stay fluid. Stay soft weary. Stay wrong. Stay pain. Stay beauty as the pain of the soul to eat not eat. Stay and go in a blaze not of endtime but end to ends, saying thank you for the spirit blitz now finished.

You Bunnies, You Will Just Have To Wait

But not if I'm gone.

≈

In the end
has anyone seen my bunny, it's pink,
green tummy,
and sore?

≈

Bunny's not here. Settle down.

≈

Bunny's settle down more bunny.

≈

Quality Street shower. The Celador
said yesyoucan, which previously on we already
like the Tibetan monks the coach seal, or the life of the towers

≈

and time it kicked the bucket
ball Charlie, yours famine exports, yours bunny voice, yours in a
world without porn

≈

kiss me
push off. We'll gain
again, come ere, there's the
psycho infant, there's the paw

≈

alife
I guess it's time
through Black Champagne previously I had
for you
a love beyond the world for you
amid the tinsel, the tickets. Must
everyone else wanted everyone else to kill
I was yes wan
to the bed spread UFO suspended on the
Devil's Tower, toys obsessed with

≈

heart you wanted
to love
to lick a it just didn't work
[. . . . .]

≈

UNBEAUTITUDE ON THE THIRD FLOOR IN COLOURS

while you were in love with Big Bird he was sick
of everyone, but he was sick of everyone

you bunnies, you will

on the slow train to Accrington Stanley,
lashes lengthened to infinity, a robin whooshes
BANG! into the bullet hole;
     the ice cream van
full of magical shit rainbows over the worry dolls . . .

     Tibetan coach steams in
says push hostility's flower's darker than the backward moon,
literary autism a dialectic complicated as the Daleks.

Bunny, stop.

Andre Brasil

Life's gimp I got tweeted to Bishopsgate all the hash tags going buzzwire
   the world language of world death
     and moving from number twenty seven to twenty three

Bunny Guinness on the shelter belt. It's literally
   everything prolonged and pro-anorexia,
     by crash dieting on everything

the refusenik affirmation that I can
   have a cat
     or fuck dazzling pessimism actually

have a cat, or rip the wrapper.
   I'll let you go then, I found a way to tie a scarf,
     I tickled a button, but first

the prolongation: *lay down by my side, she said, before we go,*
   and I sort of thought of Forward Intelligence. But what was important,
     though properly mysterious, was the note at the end of

the prolongation. It was as if I gave a prolongation that also had to
   contain within it, finally, a false note, and it was this false note,
     like an almost inaudible diamond at the end of something

unending, when she becomes something else, that saved her,
   and allowed me to lose her completely, losing even the loss itself.
     I remembered then that I used to ask for extra homework.

'May that I never be separated, not without you anyway.' Staved off
    absolute mortality, by a noglove. The model's in a velvet vault.
        Love too much. Lend some sugar. Give no energy to sin. Shakespearian.

Again and just so much in the last few years changed
    there's an almost eidetic 'Ballstack' on vision goggles. The world.
        I've been sick. I'm getting better. All the world's

love songs are the same. Take your magic mirror and stick it
    to the dumbass exodus all around, and I was wrong, so wrong,
        to need to make a beautiful explosive thing to make up

for everything and everyone. Forget love, and think of
    when I was wrong I was wrong
        and roll up the cradle when I'm done.

Get out of my car, into my dreams. This is the sound of
    the airplane century sent up by Jesus Everything
        love itself congealed in stupid maps

I make for everyone right up against the end of
    tweeters move easy free in 'sweetheart sorrow'
        the mutilated heart a hacky sack sung to the tune of

Martillion Fedex, or for the cold prefer
    a Nicole Fahri mink hot water bottle
        or big fat titty, or get out of my dreams into my

t a certain angle yrs the body responsible for continuous orgasm
   face really awkward and squishy right after sex, the ugliness
      she loved me for. Now get into that. *Milchsatt*, I was wrong. My orgasm

ce make it the object. It will shine us. It makes *Poltergeist*
   look like *The Shining*. Who are you in love with now
      the whole world, as promised.

njoy what else there is. The image is not worth watching.
   Bingo, poliomyelitis, face cream, in everyone this one chance,
      just one, this indifference to life, in love

carnate in a freeze dryer. The O transcript counts 7 to 8. He is
   right. This is it. All weeds are with us forever. It's almost
      unbearable, the Edenic impetus, the way he avoids

he void the way tatters survive the jelly, like a thousand
   little coins collected at every ploom. Vampire
      is. Vampire got crocheted up. Vampire that

ly dresses the window. Cracked wind blower
   how you only got three must-haves. Gone and done
      and got trapped up, afflicted by this been-there-

ne-everything *Weltschmerz*, and all the waxwork servants to keep
   you company. I am, bounce-irreversible,
      starting. Sun-dried muscle shells: like glass. Better than

bubble wrap. Little does the water know.
  Grow bags at the summit. Hash tag 20. Love of cardboard answers
    a truncheon lopes to heaven in a sly moment of refund

kindness, just before the Vertigo falls, a false fall,
  without waiting for anybody, with a large bag full of truncheons,
    full of an unidentifiable young body, identified now,

a body carrying a heavy bag, with a large man inside
  carrying a heavy bag, doing crack,
    vulnerable and snow white across memorious grounds,

as in Claudio in Minas Gerais where only
  nicknames in the phonebook, buttered through in the promised tours
    of the time of times which the rembobinez *interrupts,*

until Tatters, in the friend's house, born bulky,
  walking on an endless afternoon, on an eternal road, or rather
    only floating, floating, but not progressed in the zonal pips

because he was not walking, but bouncing,
  going somewhere along the road but he was not going to where that somewhere is,
    because not only did he not say anything and not say anything dumb

or a foreign one, a stranger with sketches at the end because
  they do not ask, not lost, but lost in the world, as if eating his own sex he becomes
    a cylindrical monk, perhaps an angel, or a hedgehog with ramplights,

or another giant spider, or another werewolf, a disembodied eye
  shimmying through the air, or maybe a fluffier, or a murderer
    of larger butter, thinking and speaking only of the butter,

seeing only the butter, and with a large and heavy and bulky bag,
  perhaps speaking only the language of feet, perhaps love, a little later,
    perhaps for the dumb animals perhaps he now lives with,

only living with them at last, the baby anteater
  won't leave his side, it's like a shell, like glass that sticks to his feet,
    and as the thunder of the afternoon, the cloud faces, the pissant,

and then the curtains fall, the sound of the heel clicks into change
  on the long slow sloop full of pain, and full of cardboard, inside the big heavy
    bag he carts, it's as if

as if he's about
  to bounce into   in there, forever
    surrounded by cardboard truncheons, and a basketful of candy

for tips for the netto kafe nanmin, *on this free the* Hikikomori *quest,*
  like a child who has never left home, a trouser soap
    feeling the way the camera does in the bag about the trousers,

feeling the way the trouser shop does about the game quest,
  the way Andre Brasil feels about Brazil, the way the twixter
    and the neet feel about the word bump that it is

an eagerness to watch volleyball entirely silent, but not sad,
  insinuating rather a blessing, as if he was saying everything is fine
    without sex, this voluminous walk it has destroyed all other walks,

flooding the world without words, shit, rain, trouser rain, neobaroque boredom,
  unable to escape the bathroom, never mind the new net casque,
    where he would like to live and 'bomb' come bouncing back

now is your time bag heavy and bulky, go find that young prince
  does not appear to know the tennis player. Dances discos they fall in love
    on camels, or the disk that only goes forward. It's no longer

a question to say everyone I loved little wound-fodder. That
  at least. Unzip
    the surrogate sunrise wound. Ta

S. Feline Marge. Was summat
  wrong? Just think about Daley Thompson,
    the pitter of his little feet, he doesn't even have a knighthood. Poetry,

justice. The visually impaired 200 metre guide runner. So many
  lost children in films # some text missing #

Lava Music

With its nose taped at dusk it began
to rub the bed of lackadaisical white
wood and when rubbing the plates
the bed sighed.

∾

We are in the middle of the
hippo-flaxen ark, you surf milk
in a milk-sided vixen, uptie your
knots like Formby sidling reforming
one last crack.

∾

Why is it you are
the only one
smutty enough
in that anorexic light
to that contradict against variety,
to that size up, the beloved fucked
by thick-belted ears, in a special fur
urn
    left over.

Fuck me backwards the key flagship stupid
gathering garbage capsizes past dust pops
on the nit ladder gutted, three slim
pence holding your hand into
dayglo.

~

Does not stop,
does dummy wrings its hands love
with crisps out the bees lid bleeding
anacoluthic sweat. The kids
bleed too,
kangaroos also.

~

Sissy fits tight love into a humpty free
fire. A blaze of sissies quakes across
Tommy steps had no sex, pain slaps
anonymous.

But then the next day:

The moon sails backwards to the wound,
the land wags at the animal-blight.

      It is as if, it as if is, it, as if you were
where announce an umpteenth star cup.
Missed you start.

≈

The wound wax scribes yawns
misses everything. Send the
scar up over out. While it crashes
to flower of chocolate ray island,
dash around and round turning
fight with mushrooms nerd glee.

≈

The mushroom dash jumps
skims over the earth tube, maintains long haul
dash state, but you think that it is that the
similar mechanism to that,
rallying, starting, don't you think,
it increases? It is good thing. Because I see
the world land, for a while Monkeytronic
it is being completed. So it is
of mint eyes fall.

Yatsuchiyama it was I who do not
have the fact that from in 2 it is defeated
by the Mali car but looking at this sight,
you were surprised. Existence of the mini-turbo
and the little was known for the first time
scar-tight.

Disney Roofs

Wisping, ammazzaloroso, hitched onto
a little pianism, a tender
nothing, noted, given up, said aloud

for fear of immodesty in not saying.

2

To the moon snoring an amen-
cycle gargantuan tease
that that ghostthing says

it's too much, forehead
bleeding. Tinbats
for that.

3

Manic liebsflowermilk of word ghouls, put paper on floor
print life, um, unlikely words is what I only love.

4

Unlikely love story solid bites. I lived as a kid pen scraps for mountain daylight time so close to Disneyland I could sit on my roof and watch Tinkerbell fly through the night sky. Love sneezed in your mouth *then*, but note to pieces the sudden joy of Aunty Pam making it to Tesco's in her slippers.

5

Harmless delight mindfluke
take it easy, in hip pain
is no small madness to say

the call of deep-bell cells
their confused resurrection
bleat, in there there is

simple affirmation.
The drowning polar bear sings
quietly putting it away

of lists of things usual:
Animalympics, stiletto skids,
Braziliaria, the clock with the Dresden singers.

6

A cannot star unfolds drowsily, early spring precommencing like a series of books each more affirmative than the last. Star happiness in matter story. A tiny amorous balance, that's all, love's lore strips softer now, is over, instead memorise jokes when high *so that*, so that the flags in the mirror snore.

7

But brass soloists light sad bread sounds hint Jane's part of the squirrel was filmed. Mr Joyboy is aglitter with mush, afto sleep takes him sunny side of sun. Sullivan particular local sad about costume details, so nice so quiet, like snow football drunk.

8

I have not slept since we drew
them. It cannot be erased

along with this paper? Stretch
kill, the rictus smiles, at
the top or bottom of the LA

hills a bike thrown down
there is a wasted pizza, swings
swinging, the afterparty channel

rewinds a sorer point.

9

It is a pressure, with it they are
suffering suckers, go down

easy, no Christmas tree music
to make us wake. Even so it's as ever
never, a locksmith on the loose.

There's stuff coming up. Whipped
chimps have their days now, a croquet
champ's buried mouth speaks out

too slowly of dark family
hide-and-seek. From the window
a bag of crisps emerges.

CPSIA information can be obtained
at www.ICGtesting.com
Printed in the USA
LVOW13s1607211216
518287LV00011B/1307/P